Learning About Life Cycles

The Life Cycle of an

Owl

Ruth Thomson

PowerKiDS
press

New York

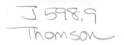

Published in 2009 by The Rosen Publishing Group Inc.
29 East 21st Street, New York, NY 10010

First Edition

Editor: Victoria Brooker
Designer: Simon Morse
Consultant: David Ramsden, Senior Conservation Officer,
The Barn Owl Trust

Library of Congress Cataloging-in-Publication Data

Thomson, Ruth, 1949-
   The life cycle of an owl / Ruth Thomson.
        p. cm. — (Learning about life cycles)
   Includes index.
   ISBN 978-1-4358-2833-9 (library binding)
   ISBN 978-1-4358-2883-4 (paperback)
   ISBN 978-1-4358-2889-6 (6-pack)
   1. Owls—Life cycles—Juvenile literature. I. Title.
   QL696.S8T46 2009
   598.9'7—dc22

                                   2008026176

Manufactured in China

Photographs: 7 Birdman Photographer/Alamy;
20-21, 23 (br) Michael Callan/Frank Lane Picture
Agency; cover (cr), 12, 23 (tr) DK Limited/Kim
Taylor/Corbis: COVER (cr); Cover (main)
Val Duncan/Kenebec Images/Alamy;
8 Lisa Moore/Alamy; 18 Michael
Roas/Frank Lane Picture Agency; 14
Michael Leech/OSF/Photolibrary Group; 3,
4, 5, 6, 7, 9, 10, 11, 13, 15, 16, 17, 19, 22
naturepl.com

Web Sites

Contents

Owls live here

This owl lives near farms and grassland. At dawn and dusk, it glides low over fields in search of mice, shrews, and **voles**.

What is an owl?

An owl is a bird of **prey**. This means it hunts small animals for food. It has very good eyesight and hearing. It flies silently and pounces on animals with its feet. It usually swallows them whole.

There are many types of owl.
This book is about a barn owl.

large head that can turn all the way around and upside-down

large, round eyes that help the owl to see in dim light

disk of flat feathers that direct sounds to the ears

soft, fringed feathers for quiet flight

hooked beak for tearing up food

sharp, curved **claws** for gripping prey

Finding a mate

In the spring, males and females **roost** near their nest. The male offers the female food to make her plump before they **mate**.

The pair chase around, **screeching** loudly. They also **preen** each other and rub cheeks.

9

Laying eggs

The female lays her eggs on
a soft layer of **pellets**. She lays
between three and seven eggs.
These are laid two days apart.

The mother sits on her eggs
to keep them warm. She turns
them from time to time. The
male brings her food to eat.

Hatching

After a month, the chicks **hatch**, one every two days. They scrape the eggshell until it cracks open. They push their way out.

Owl chicks are blind and weak.
They are covered with only
a thin coat of fluffy **down**.

2
days

Chicks

The chicks stay near their
mother to keep warm.

1
week

The father brings food for them all.
The mother tears it into small
pieces and feeds the chicks.
They grow a thicker fluffy coat.

Owlets

The owlets get bigger and stronger. They begin to run and practice pouncing.

5 weeks

Feathers start to grow on the owlets' wings.

8 weeks

9 weeks

Soon, they are feathered all over. They practice flapping their wings.

10
weeks

Time to fly

Now the owlets are strong enough to fly. At first, they take short flights.

When the owlets can fly well, they hunt for their own food. They **roost** in nearby trees.

12 weeks

Leaving home

There is not enough food to feed the whole family in the same area. The owlets have to fly away.

14 weeks

They often travel many miles before they find a new place to **roost** and hunt.

21

1
year

Adult owl

Now the owl is fully grown.
In the spring, it will find a **mate**
and produce young of its own.

Owl life cycle

Eggs
The mother lays
three to seven eggs,
one every two days.

Chicks
The chicks **hatch**
one at a time.

Adult owls
The adult owls find a **mate**
and produce young of
their own.

Owlets
The owlets grow feathers and learn
to fly. They leave their parents and
find a home of their own.

Glossary and Further Information

claw a curved, pointed nail at the end of a bird or animal's foot

down the light, soft feathers of chicks

hatch to come out of an egg

mate when a male and female join together to produce young

pellet a small, hard ball that contains the bones and fur of the animals the owl has eaten. It comes out of the owl's beak.

preen when a bird smooths and cleans its feathers

prey the creatures that a bird or an animal hunts for food

roost to sleep

screech to make a loud, harsh cry

vole a small, furry animal similar to a mouse

Books

All About Owls
by Jim Arnosky (Scholastic, 1999)

What is a Life Cycle?
by Bobbie Kalman (Crabtree Publishing, 1998)

Index